How To Draw Cats and Kittens

By Karen McKee

INTRODUCTION

Follow the simple steps in this book and soon you'll be drawing all your favorite cats and kittens.

SUPPLIES

NUMBER 2 PENCILS	FELT-TIP PEN
SOFT ERASER	COLORED PENCILS,
DRAWING PAPER	MARKERS,
OR PAD	OR CRAYONS

HOW TO START

Most drawings in this book are broken down into four steps. Start drawing each cat by following and sketching the first step. Many of the lines or guidelines that you draw will be erased, so they should be lightly drawn. (Dotted lines shown will also be erased.)

Draw the second step over the first one. Then, blend all your lines and shapes together, erasing any guidelines you no longer need. Finally, add details and shading.

Remember to keep erasing and drawing until you are satisfied with the way your cat or kitten looks. When your drawing is complete, you may outline or color it with markers, colored pencils, or crayons.

Most drawings of cats begin with circular and oval shapes for the head and face, and large oval shapes for the main parts of the body. After the shapes are connected, the legs and paws, ears, nose, eyes, and tail are added. When all the shapes have been smoothly blended together and the guidelines have been erased, short jagged lines are drawn around the cat's body outline to make it look furry. Lastly, whiskers, special body markings, and any other details are added to complete the drawing.

These are the cats and kittens that are in this book.

SIAMESE

DEVON REX

PERSIAN

AMERICAN SHORTHAIR

ABYSSINIAN

RUSSIAN BLUE

MANX

CHEEETAH

TABBY CAT

BURMESE

CALICO

LION CUB

KITTEN

KITTEN

LONGHAIRED SILVER TABBY

SIAMESE

Popular, blue-eyed Siamese cats have tan or cream-colored fur with darker color on their face, tail, legs, and paws. These dark areas are called "points." There are four kinds: blue point, lilac point, chocolate point, and seal point.

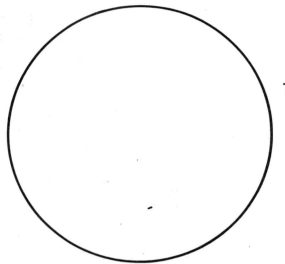

1. Begin by drawing a circular shape.

Note: Always draw your guidelines lightly in steps 1 and 2 — it will be easier to erase them later.

2. Next add the other basic shapes for the ears, eyes, and mouth.

3. Add the nose, and details to the eyes. Start defining and shaping the head and face. Siamese cats have longer faces than most other breeds. Add lines to suggest the body.

Add

Add

4. This Siamese has dark brown fur on its face and head. Carefully color it, leaving white strands of hair and fur visible, as shown. For the final touch, add the whiskers.

TABBY CAT

Tabby is a coat pattern, not a breed. Stripes are the main coat pattern among these cats. Tabbies' color variety is endless, and their affectionate personalities make them popular house pets.

1. Begin by lightly sketching a circle for the head and two ovals for the body, as shown.

2. Add the ears, mouth, leg and paw, and tail. Erase any unnecessary guidelines as you go along.

3. Continue to erase guidelines as you blend all the shapes together. Add the eyes and nose, and start adding details. Use a wavy, jagged line to make the tabby look furry.

Keep drawing and erasing until your tabby looks "just right."

4. Complete your drawing by adding whiskers, other details, and the tabby's stripes.

AMERICAN SHORTHAIR

American shorthaired cats are large, usually friendly, and gentle. Their good nature makes them popular to keep as pets. Their fur can be any color or pattern.

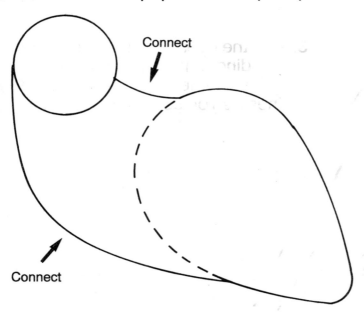

Connect

Connect

1. Lightly sketch a circle for the head and a large oval for the hindquarter. Connect the shapes with two curved lines, forming the body.

Note: The basic body guideline shapes will be different if the cat is in another position.

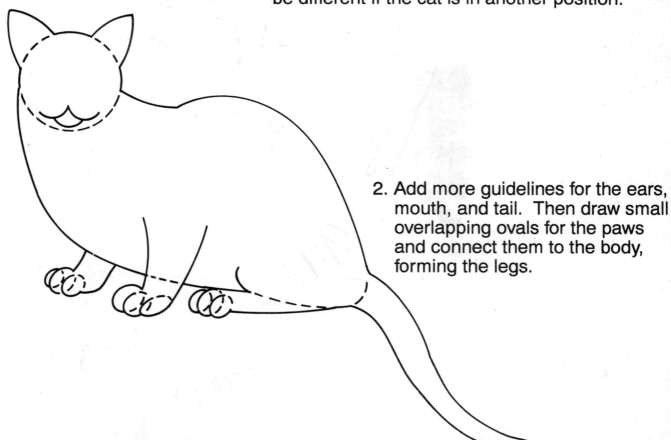

2. Add more guidelines for the ears, mouth, and tail. Then draw small overlapping ovals for the paws and connect them to the body, forming the legs.

3. Add the eyes and nose, and start blending, shaping, and curving the body lines. Erase your guide-lines as you go along.

If you're not satisfied with the way any part of your drawing looks, erase it and draw it again. Remember, practice makes perfect!

4. Add the whiskers, lots of shading, and all the little details that will give your drawing a finished look.

CALICO

A calico cat has irregular patches of black, orange, and white-colored fur. This unusual looking cat can be either a shorthair or longhair.

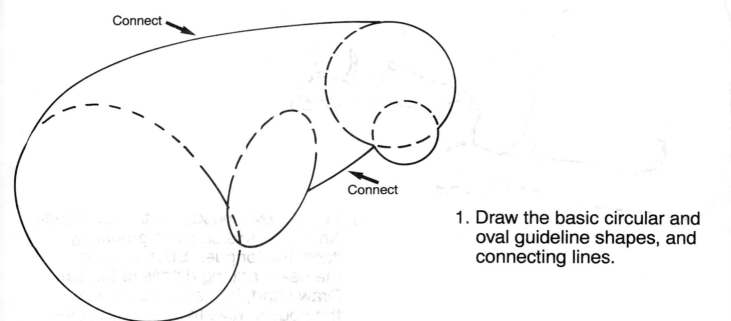

Connect

Connect

1. Draw the basic circular and oval guideline shapes, and connecting lines.

Always draw your guidelines lightly in steps 1 and 2 — it will be easier to erase them later.

2. Add the ears, legs and paws, and tail. Blend the lines and shapes together, erasing unnecessary guidelines.

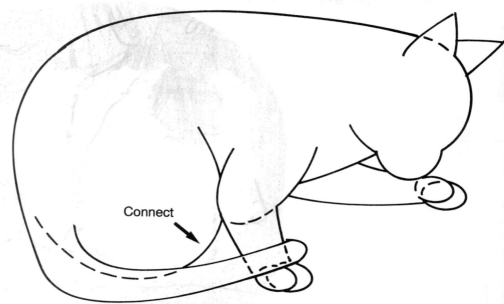

Connect

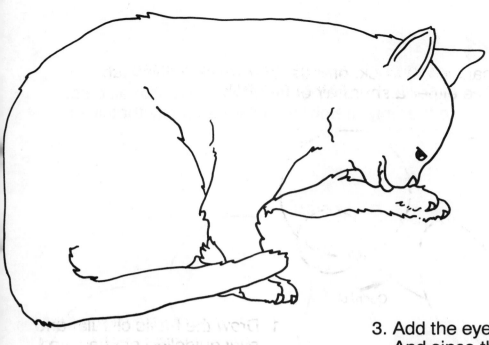

3. Add the eye, nose, mouth, and claws.
   And since this calico is grooming
   itself, the tongue. Start shaping
   the head, adding details to the ear.
   Draw short, jagged lines around
   the body to give the cat a furry look.

4. Add the whiskers and other details.
   When your drawing is complete,
   color the calico's fur with areas
   of white, orange, and black.

LION CUB

There are usually one to three lion cubs in a litter. The cubs, like all cats, are helpless at birth. Lions are the only members of the cat family that live in groups, called prides.

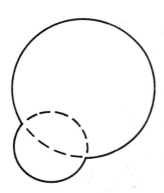

1. Begin with two overlapping circles for the head.

2. Sketching lightly, add a large oval guideline for the body and three oval guidelines for the upper legs.

Add

3. Add the ears, mouth, lower part of the legs, and paws, erasing unneeded guidelines as you go.

Keep erasing guidelines as you refine your drawing.

4. Add the eyes, nose, tail, details to the mouth, and the right hind leg. Then with a squiggly or jagged line go over the outline of the cub to give it a furry look.

Add

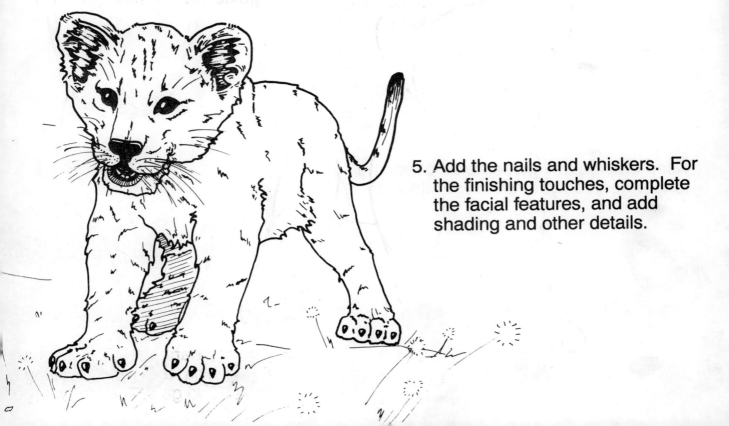

5. Add the nails and whiskers. For the finishing touches, complete the facial features, and add shading and other details.

DEVON REX

This rare and unusual cat comes from England and has curly fur. The fur can be almost any color or pattern.

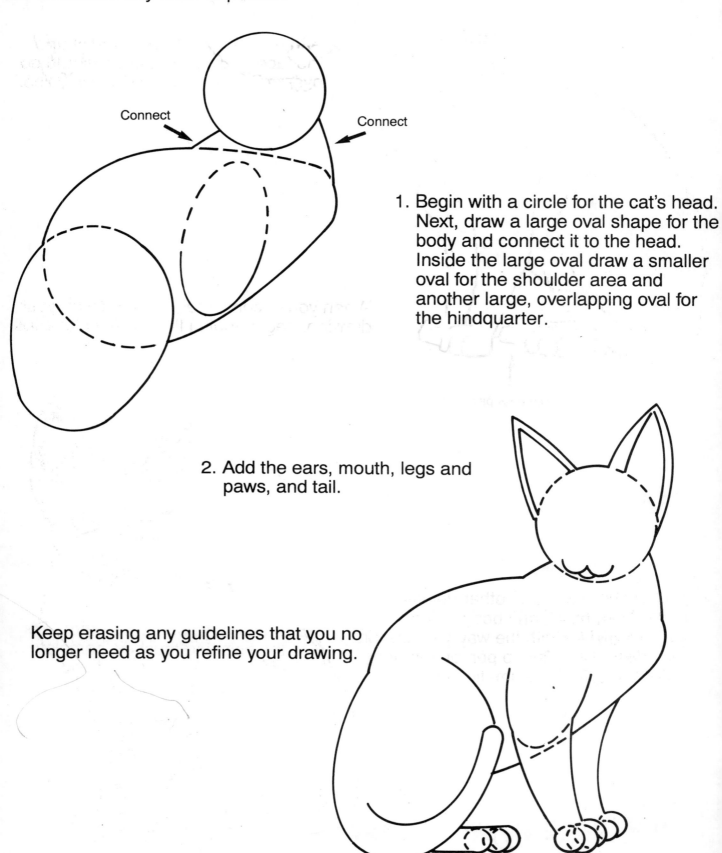

Connect

Connect

1. Begin with a circle for the cat's head. Next, draw a large oval shape for the body and connect it to the head. Inside the large oval draw a smaller oval for the shoulder area and another large, overlapping oval for the hindquarter.

2. Add the ears, mouth, legs and paws, and tail.

Keep erasing any guidelines that you no longer need as you refine your drawing.

Add back paw

3. Add the nose and eyes, and shape the face. Complete the paws and go over the entire body with a wavy line.

When you're completely satisfied with your drawing, begin adding the finishing touches.

4. Add the whiskers and other details to the face, head, and body. When you're satisfied with the way your Devon rex looks, use a felt-tip pen on the body outline to give it a dramatic look.

RUSSIAN BLUE

This elegant shorthaired cat has long, slim legs which are slightly longer in the back than in the front. Russian blues are sweet natured and intelligent cats.

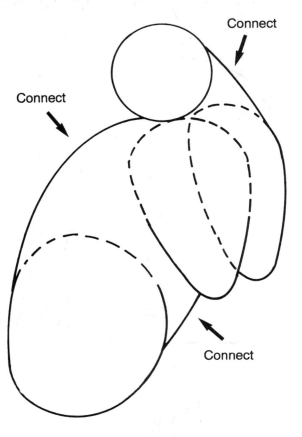

1. Lightly draw the basic body shapes for the head, shoulder areas, and hind-quarter, and connect them.

Remember: It's easy to draw any cat or kitten if you break it down into simple shapes first.

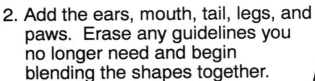

2. Add the ears, mouth, tail, legs, and paws. Erase any guidelines you no longer need and begin blending the shapes together.

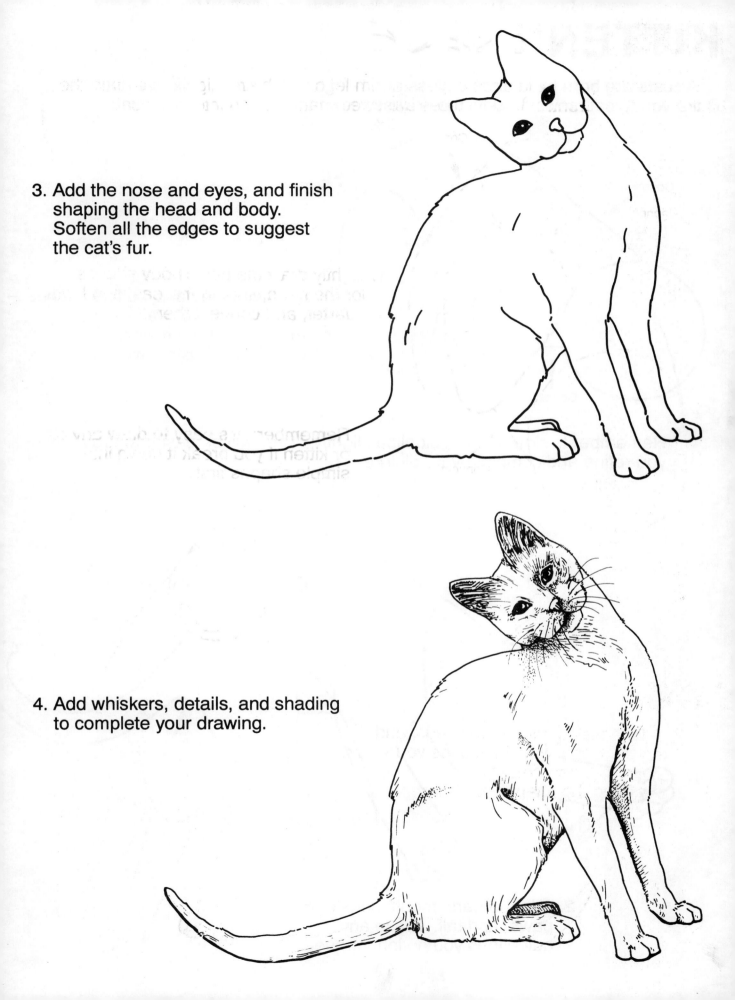

3. Add the nose and eyes, and finish
   shaping the head and body.
   Soften all the edges to suggest
   the cat's fur.

4. Add whiskers, details, and shading
   to complete your drawing.

KITTEN

All cats are born blind and helpless and feed only on milk for six to eight weeks. But a young cat grows quickly and, in just a few months, will be on its own.

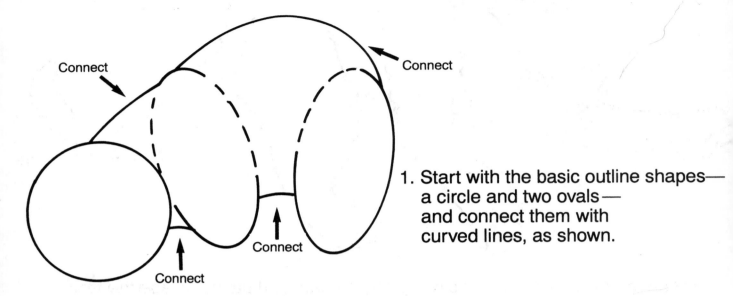

1. Start with the basic outline shapes—a circle and two ovals—and connect them with curved lines, as shown.

Remember to draw these guidelines lightly. They will be easier to erase as you refine and complete your picture.

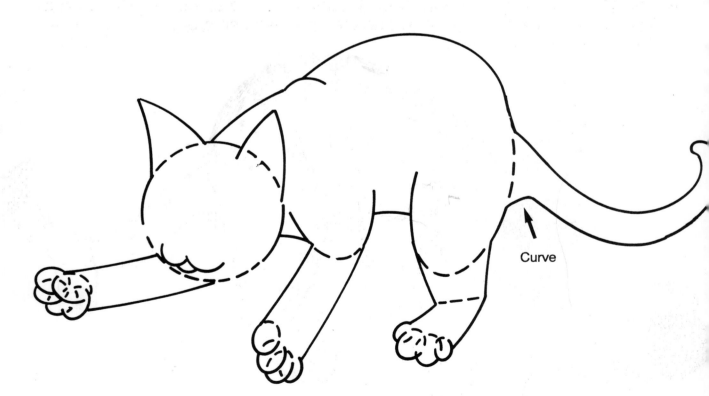

2. Add the ears, mouth, legs and paws, and tail. Erase any guidelines you no longer need.

3. Add the nose and eyes, and complete the ears and paws. Shape the face and head, and begin adding the furry outline.

4. This kitten is a striped tabby. Use shading to create stripes all over its body. They can be any color. Finally, add the whiskers and a big ball of yarn for this frisky kitten to play with.

MANX

Manx cats have no tails, and although their fur is short, it is thicker than that of other shorthaired cats. They come from the Isle of Man, a small island in the Irish Sea.

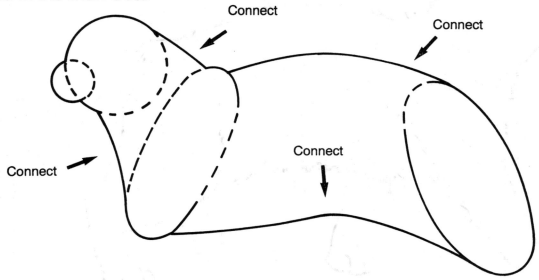

1. Draw a circle for the head and a smaller, overlapping one for the nose and mouth area. Add ovals for the shoulder and hindquarter and connect the shapes together.

Remember: Guidelines should always be lightly drawn.

2. Add guidelines for the ear, paws and legs, and begin erasing the guidelines within the body. Blend the lines together into a smooth body shape.

Now that the basic shapes have been completed, you can begin to refine your drawing.

3. Complete the ear and add the eye and nose. Draw short broken, or jagged, lines around the body to make the manx look furry. Complete the feet and legs and begin adding details.

4. Add the whiskers and all the final details to complete your picture. A Manx can be almost any color, even striped like a tabby cat.

ABYSSINIAN

Each hair of an Abyssinian's fur is several different colors. It starts out silvery, then gradually changes from brown to black.

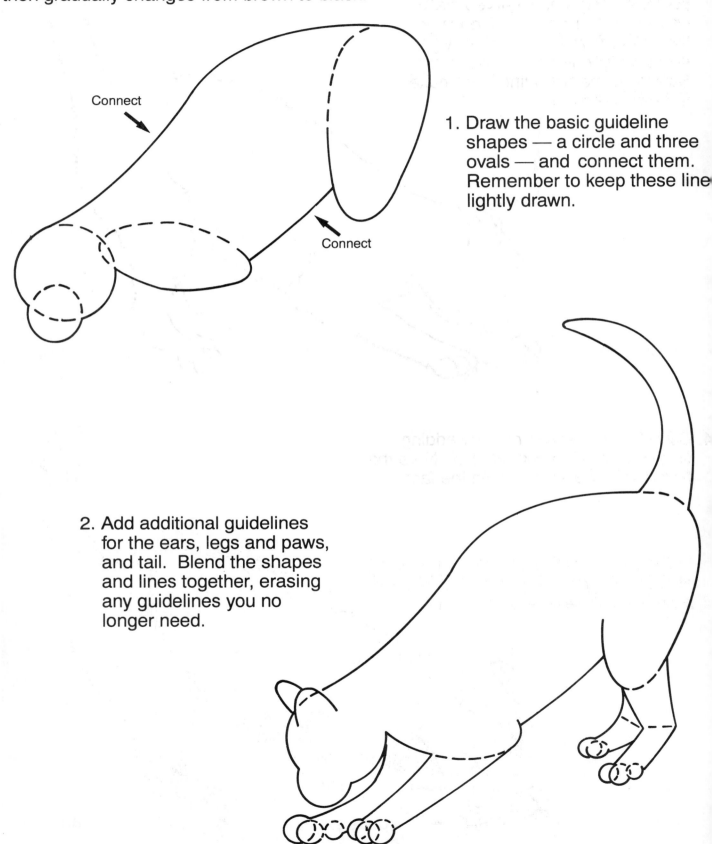

Connect

Connect

1. Draw the basic guideline shapes — a circle and three ovals — and connect them. Remember to keep these line lightly drawn.

2. Add additional guidelines for the ears, legs and paws, and tail. Blend the shapes and lines together, erasing any guidelines you no longer need.

3. Add the eye, nose, and mouth. Shape the head and define the paws, adding small, curved claws on the front ones. Then, go over the cat's entire body outline with short, jagged lines to suggest fur. Softening the body lines will make the cat look furry.

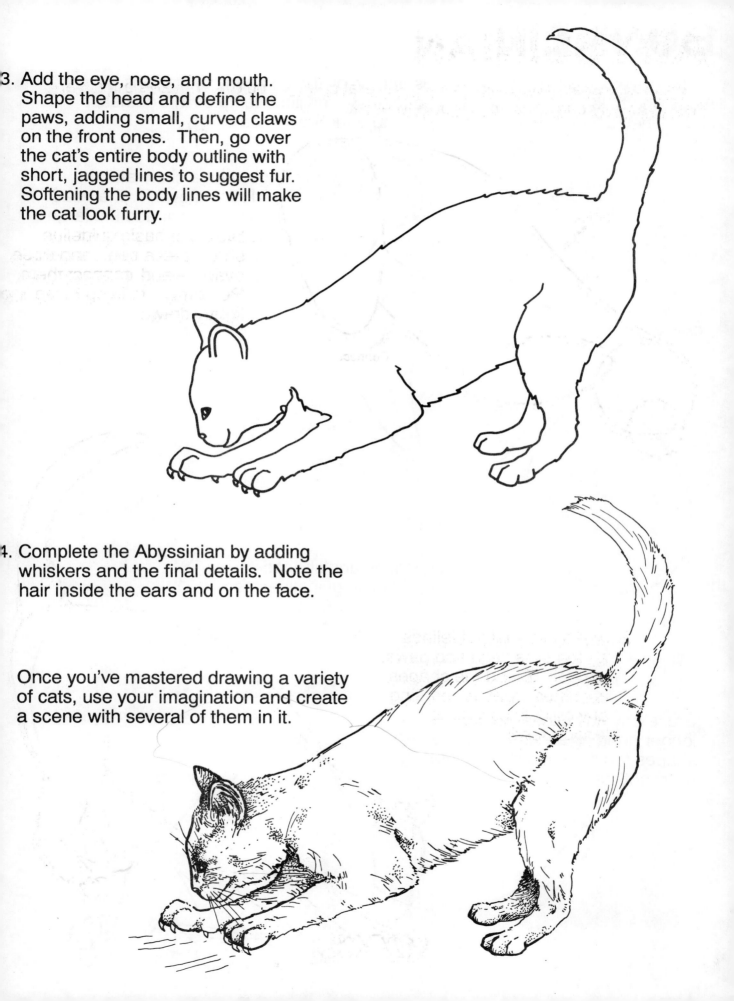

4. Complete the Abyssinian by adding whiskers and the final details. Note the hair inside the ears and on the face.

Once you've mastered drawing a variety of cats, use your imagination and create a scene with several of them in it.

BURMESE

Burmese cats have sweet natures and enjoy the company of humans. According to legend, they were used to guard religious temples in Southeast Asia. They usually have golden eyes and dark brown coats.

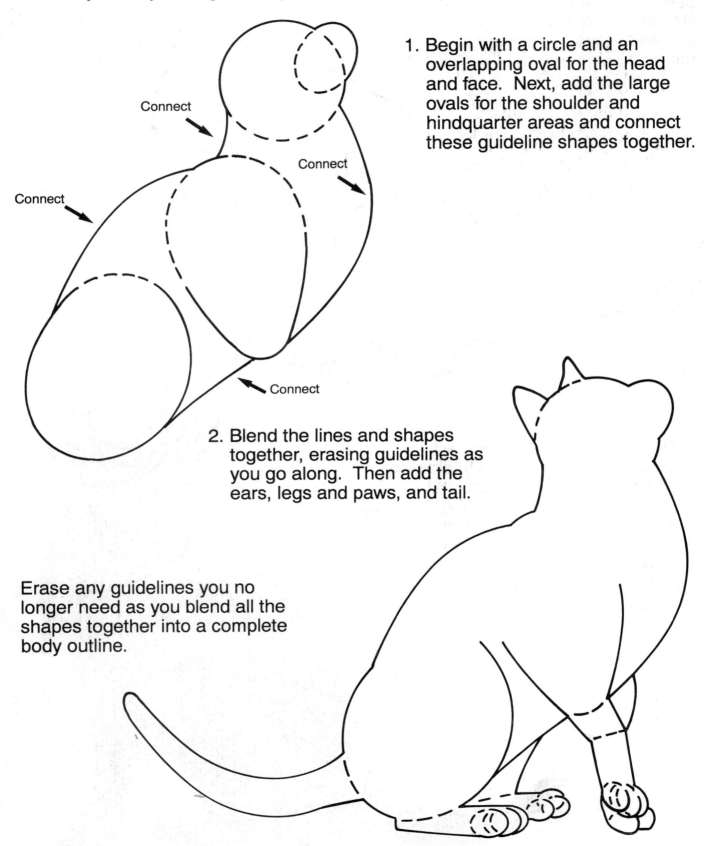

1. Begin with a circle and an overlapping oval for the head and face. Next, add the large ovals for the shoulder and hindquarter areas and connect these guideline shapes together.

2. Blend the lines and shapes together, erasing guidelines as you go along. Then add the ears, legs and paws, and tail.

Erase any guidelines you no longer need as you blend all the shapes together into a complete body outline.

3. Add the eye, nose, and mouth, and begin shaping the legs, paws, ears, and tail. Remember to use short, jagged lines for the outline of the body.

Note: Make sure that you are satisfied with the way your drawing looks before going to step #4.

4. Carefully add lots of shading to the dark brown Burmese. Remember to leave some white strands showing, which will make the cat look furry.

PERSIAN

This longhaired Asian cat is famous for its long, fluffy fur. It has a round face, round eyes, snub nose, and small ears. Persians come in many different colors.

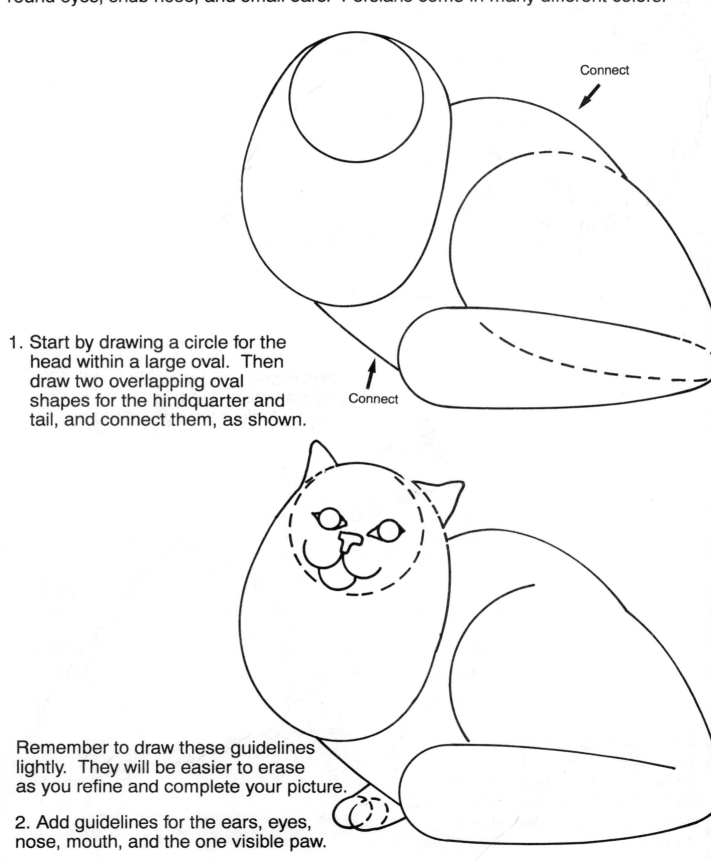

Connect

Connect

1. Start by drawing a circle for the head within a large oval. Then draw two overlapping oval shapes for the hindquarter and tail, and connect them, as shown.

Remember to draw these guidelines lightly. They will be easier to erase as you refine and complete your picture.

2. Add guidelines for the ears, eyes, nose, mouth, and the one visible paw.

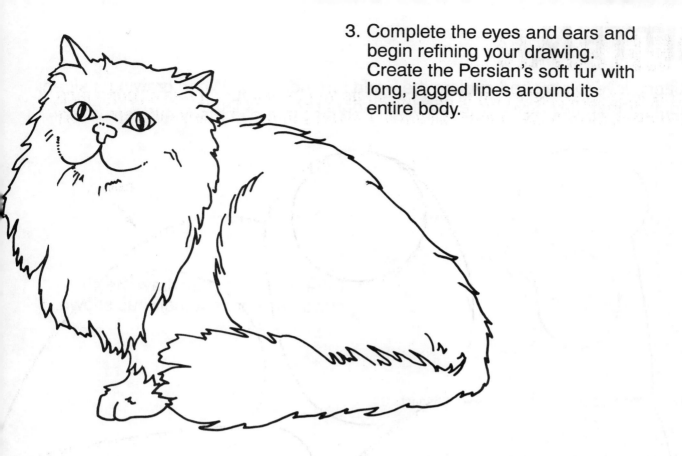

3. Complete the eyes and ears and begin refining your drawing. Create the Persian's soft fur with long, jagged lines around its entire body.

Keep erasing and sketching until you are satisfied with the way your drawing looks before going to step #4.

4. Continue adding more flowing and jagged lines to give the Persian a full, longhaired furry look. Add whiskers and final details, and this show cat is ready to pose.

KITTEN

Kittens love to play and explore the world around them. When drawing a kitten, remember that they have large heads and ears but small faces.

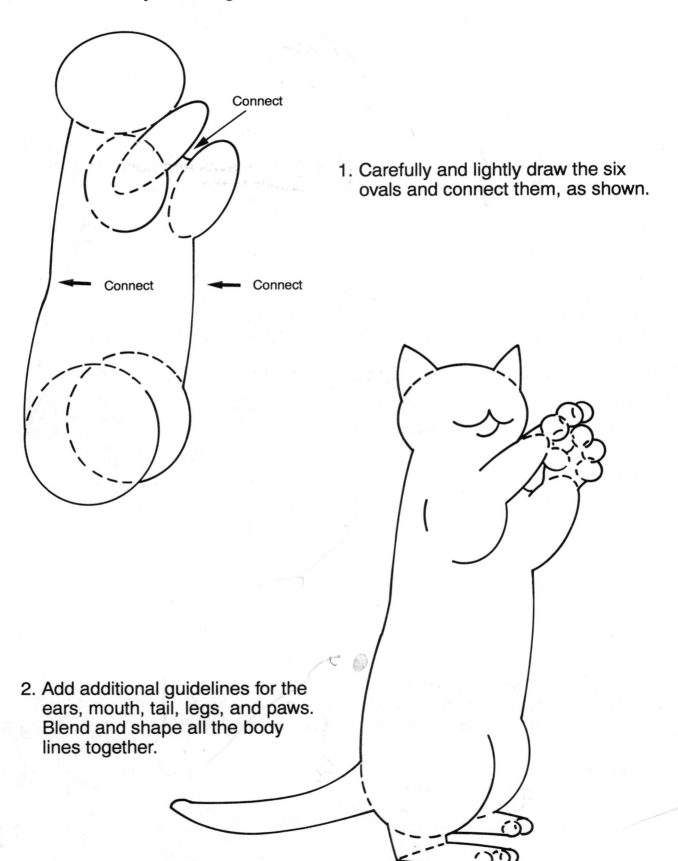

Connect

Connect

Connect

1. Carefully and lightly draw the six ovals and connect them, as shown.

2. Add additional guidelines for the ears, mouth, tail, legs, and paws. Blend and shape all the body lines together.

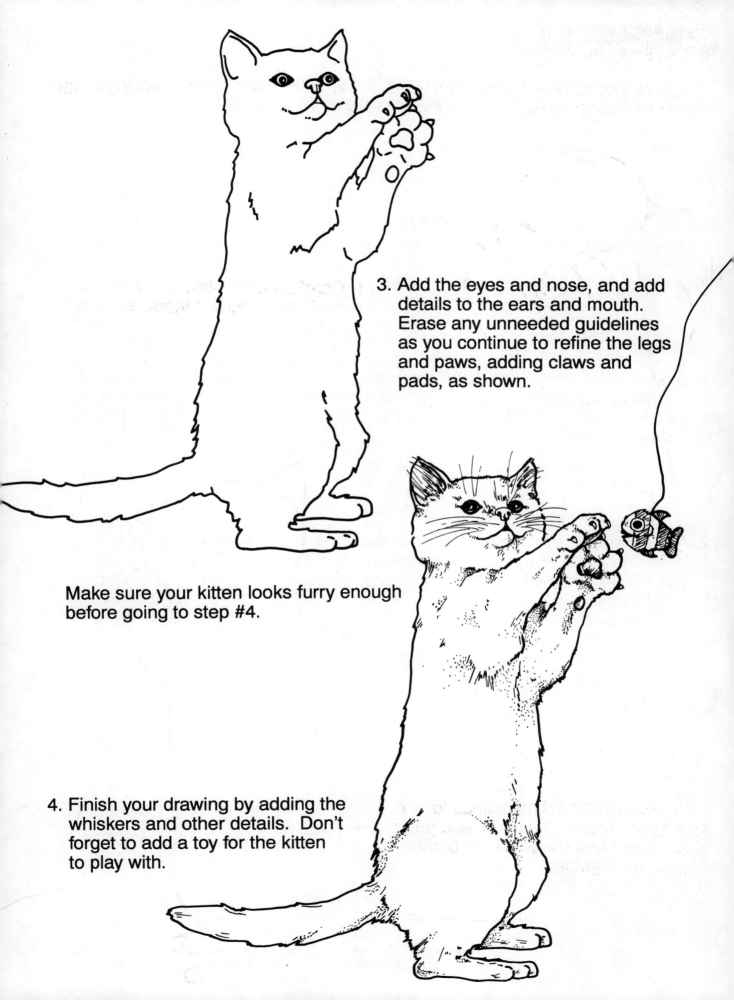

3. Add the eyes and nose, and add details to the ears and mouth. Erase any unneeded guidelines as you continue to refine the legs and paws, adding claws and pads, as shown.

Make sure your kitten looks furry enough before going to step #4.

4. Finish your drawing by adding the whiskers and other details. Don't forget to add a toy for the kitten to play with.

CHEETAH

The cheetah is the fastest land animal in the world. Its streamlined body and long, slender legs enable it to run at speeds over 60 miles per hour.

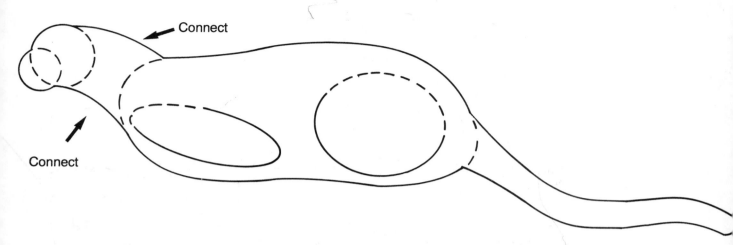

1. Draw a circle for the head and a smaller, overlapping one for the nose and mouth area. Then, create a large oval shape for the long body and connect it to the head. Add the tail. Inside the body add two oval guideline shapes for the shoulder and hindquarter.

2. Add an ear, mouth, leg and paw guidelines. Since the legs are overlapping, it's easier to start with the ones on the side of the cheetah that is closest to you. Then add the ones behind. Blend all the lines together into a smooth body shape.

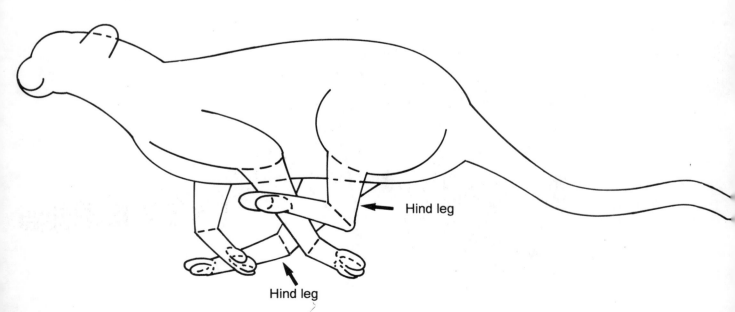

Erase any guidelines you no longer need.

3. Add the eye, nose, the tip of the second ear, and details to the face. Continue shaping all parts of the cheetah, paying close attention to the line that forms the stomach.

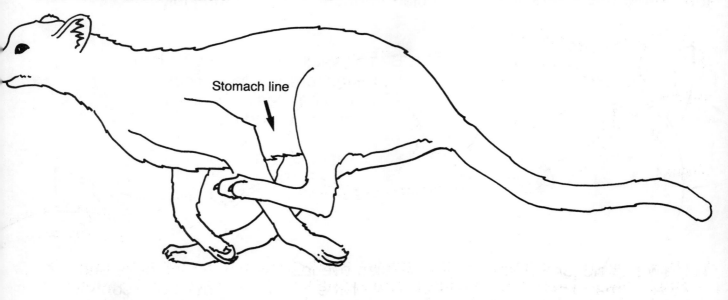

Stomach line

When you're satisfied with the way your drawing looks, start adding the final details.

4. A cheetah's tan and orange fur is covered with solid black spots. Add the spots, other details — and the whiskers.

LONGHAIRED SILVER TABBY

This spectacular looking cat has a clear silver undercoat with black tabby markings top. The tabby stripes are slightly blurred due to the extra-long fur.

1. Begin by lightly sketching a circular shape for the head. Then, add the other basic shapes for the ears, eyes, and mouth.

2. Add the nose and start adding details to the ears, eyes, and mouth. Then, frame the entire head with long, flowing fur.

Erase any guidelines you no longer need.

3. Carefully draw the final details that will make this beautiful tabby look extra fluffy. Don't forget the whiskers!

When you're satisfied with the way your picture looks, use a thicker pencil or felt-tip pen to highlight some of the lines and details.